LABS
lightweights **littermates**

sharon montrose

Stewart, Tabori & Chang

New York

Published in 2005 by
Stewart, Tabori & Chang, 115 West 18th Street, New York, NY 10011
www.abramsbooks.com

Canadian Distribution:
Canadian Manda Group, 165 Dufferin Street, Toronto, Ontario M6K 3H6 Canada

Library of Congress Cataloging-in-Publication Data
Montrose, Sharon.
Labs: lightweights-littermates / Sharon Montrose.
p. cm.
ISBN 1-58479-469-0
1. Labrador retriever—Pictorial works. I. Title
SF429.L3M66 2005
636.752'7—dc22
2005042605

Designed by Sally Ann Field
Production by Alexis Mentor

The text of this book was composed in Eatwell Skinny & Eatwell Chubby by Chank Diesel.

Printed in China

10 9 8 7 6 5 4 3 2 1

First Printing

Stewart, Tabori & Chang is a subsidiary of

LA MARTINIÈRE
GROUPE

lightweights **littermates** five weeks old

churchill **4** lbs. **12** ozs.

poco 3 lbs. 13 ozs.

gordy 5 lbs. 3ozs.

cecil 4 lbs. 8 ozs.

purcell **4** lbs. **4** ozs.

claire **4** lbs. 15 ozs.

dente **4** lbs. **3** ozs.

lightweights **littermates** three weeks old

dumont 2 lbs. 6 ozs.

lasalle 3 lbs. 4 ozs.

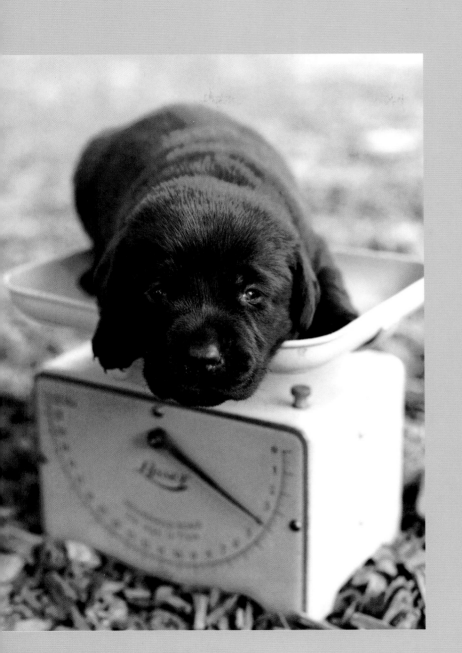

judy 3 lbs. 14 ozs.

glory 1 lb. 14 ozs.

lightweights **littermates** six weeks old

tabitha 5 lbs. 8 ozs.

peter 5 lbs. 14 ozs.

mitts 5 lbs. 3 ozs.

arrow 5 lbs. 12 ozs.

nick **5** lbs. **11** ozs.

angelus 6 lbs. 1 oz.

ashley **5** lbs. **6** ozs.

lightweights **littermates** five weeks old

dino **6** lbs. **11** ozs.

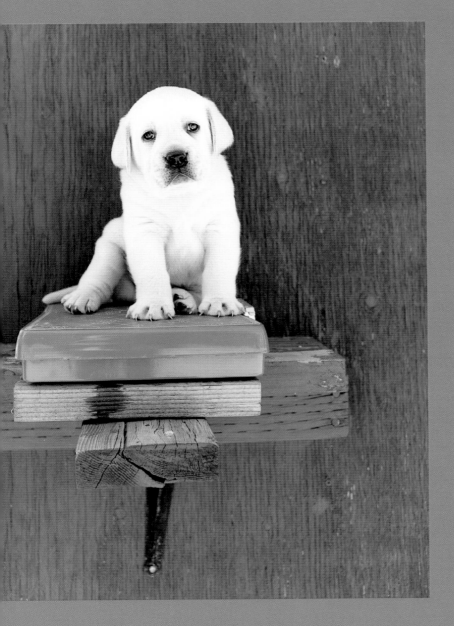

dolce **6** lbs. **3** ozs.

gepetto **6** lbs. **8** ozs.

lightweights **littermates** seven weeks old

delia **5** lbs. **13** ozs.

cocoa 6 lbs. 3 ozs.

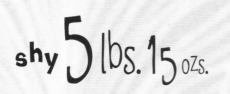

shy 5 lbs. 15 ozs.

willy 5 lbs. 2 ozs.

roger **6** lbs. **8** ozs.

cur 5 lbs. 11 ozs.

calvin 6 lbs. 8 ozs.

godiva 5 lbs. 8 ozs.

hershey **6** lbs. **9** ozs.

mirna **7** lbs. **13**ozs.

clark **8** lbs. **4** ozs.

alfred **9** lbs. **2** ozs.

vivian **8** lbs. **8** ozs.

chaplin 8 lbs. 13 ozs.

jane

hardy **9** lbs. **4** ozs.

bishop **9** lbs. **2** ozs.

slim

lightweights **littermates** six weeks old

milo **4** lbs. **8** ozs.

liv **4** lbs. 10 ozs.

reba **4** lbs. **4** ozs.

marnie 4 lbs. 3ozs.

mister 4 lbs. 7 ozs.

le-ann **4** lbs. 2ozs.

staub **4** lbs. **11**ozs.

tramp **4** lbs. **15**ozs.

With many thanks to family and friends, as always.

Also, Hendrick and Sally.

Bob Weinberg.

My literary agent, Betsy Amster.

Leslie Stoker, Beth Huseman and the whole staff at Stewart, Tabori and Chang.

Everyone at the Icon.

Craig and everyone at Photo Center.

Charles Lee.

All the adorable little puppies and their breeders.

A very special thank you to Sally Ann Field.

And, especially, Spencer Starr.

Puppies provided by:

SUSANA LABRADORS www.susanalabradors.com

SUSANA LABRADORS www.susanalabradors.com

SUSANA LABRADORS www.susanalabradors.com

LORI HANDREN

TRACEY ALBERRI www.californialabs.com

SUSANA LABRADORS www.susanalabradors.com

TUCCILLO LABS